SIXTY

Horses

by Dorothy Hinshaw Patent
photographs by William Muñoz

Lerner Publications Company • Minneapolis, Minnesota

To Sandy —DHP
For Charlotte —WM

Thanks to our series consultant, Sharyn Fenwick, elementary science/math specialist. Mrs. Fenwick was the winner of the National Science Teachers Association 1991 Distinguished Teaching Award. She also was the recipient of the Presidential Award for Excellence in Math and Science Teaching, representing the state of Minnesota at the elementary level in 1992.

The photograph on page 16 is reproduced through the courtesy of © Daniel J. Cox/ naturalexposures.com

Early Bird Nature Books were conceptualized by Ruth Berman and designed by Steve Foley. Series editor is Joelle Riley.

Lerner Publications Company
A division of Lerner Publishing Group
241 First Avenue North
Minneapolis, MN 55401 U.S.A.

Website address: www.lernerbooks.com

Library of Congress Cataloging-in-Publication Data

Patent, Dorothy Hinshaw
    Horses / by Dorothy Hinshaw Patent ; photographs by William Muñoz.
      p.   cm. — (Early bird nature books)
    Includes index.
    Summary: Describes the physical characteristics, history, and behavior of horses and discusses their interactions with humans.
    ISBN 0-8225-3045-7 (lib. bdg. : alk. paper)
    1. Horses—Juvenile literature. [1. Horses.] I. Muñoz, William, ill. II. Title. III. Series.
SF302.P373 2001
636.1—dc21   00-008-27

Manufactured in the United States of America
1 2 3 4 5 6 – JR – 06 05 04 03 02 01

Contents

Be a Word Detective

*Can you find these words as you read about the horse's life?
Be a detective and try to figure out what they mean. You
can turn to the glossary on page 46 for help.*

band	**foal**	**mare**
breeds	**graze**	**nurse**
domesticated	**herbivores**	**predators**
endangered	**hoof**	**stallion**
extinct	**mane**	

5

Horses are good runners. What do we call horses who are owned by people?

All Kinds of Horses

 Horses are beautiful animals. They have strong, sleek bodies. They move gracefully.

Most horses are owned by people. These horses are called domesticated (duh-MESS-tuh-kate-ehd) horses. What we think of as wild horses are not truly wild. They came from horses who escaped from people a long time ago. These horses are called feral horses. They live without any help from people.

Shetland ponies have long, thick hair during the winter. It keeps them warm and dry.

About 40,000 feral horses live in the western part of the United States. More than half of them live in Nevada. Most of the land there is open and unfenced. Feral horses can roam freely.

Feral horses run in open land.

It takes horses a long time to eat all the grass they need.

There are many different breeds of horses. The breeds are different colors, shapes, and sizes. But all breeds are the same species (SPEE-sheez), or kind, of animal. Horses, donkeys, zebras, and wild asses belong to the same group of animals. The scientific name for this group is *Equus* (EHK-wuhs).

Horses come in many sizes and colors.

Horses can be large or small. A horse's height is measured from the ground to the top of its shoulders. Full-grown miniature horses may be only 34 inches at the shoulder. That is about as tall as a six-year-old child. Other horses may be more than 72 inches tall. That is as tall as a tall person.

Horses come in many colors. They can be white, black, brown, or anything in between. Some horses have big spots. Other horses have little spots.

A horse's mane and tail can be the same color.
Its body can be a different color.

This horse is using its hoof to scratch an itch.

A horse's foot is called a hoof. The hoof is actually a giant toe. A horse does not stand on the flat part of its foot the way people do.
A horse walks and runs on the tips of its toes.

Horses can run fast. Their legs are long
and slender. And their leg muscles are strong.

Many horses roam free in the American West.

*This horse is alert.
Its ears are standing
straight up.*

Horses have keen senses. Their senses let them notice things quickly. Horses have a good sense of smell.

A horse's ears can move to face forward or to the sides. So horses can hear sounds from many directions.

A horse's eyes are on the sides of its head. That way, it can see dangers to its front, sides, and back.

Horses can watch for danger, even when they eat.

Mountain lions sometimes hunt horses.

   A horse's eyes, ears, and nose help to protect it from predators (PREH-duh-turz). Predators are animals who hunt and eat other animals. Mountain lions are predators who sometimes hunt horses.

Chapter 2

Horses need lots of food. What do horses eat?

Eating and Drinking

 Horses graze. When they graze, they eat grass. Horses eat bushes and wildflowers, too. Horses are herbivores (HUR-buh-vorz). Herbivores are animals who eat plants.

Horses have good teeth for grazing. Their front teeth have sharp edges for clipping tough grass. Their back teeth are heavy and wide.

These horses are grazing. They graze for many hours each day.

Horses eat about 25 pounds of grass each day.

A horse's back teeth have hard ridges for grinding the grass. Horses move their jaws from side to side to grind grass.

Water holes like this one help horses to survive.

Horses spend most of their time grazing. A medium-sized horse needs to eat about 25 pounds of grass every day. Horses also need to drink water.

Chapter 3

Horses live in family groups. What is a baby horse called?

Living Together

 A male horse is called a stallion (STAL-yun). A female horse is called a mare. A baby horse is called a foal.

Horses live together in family groups called bands. Each band has one stallion. The rest of the horses in the band are mares and their foals. A band may be as small as one stallion and one mare. Or a band may have more than twenty horses.

Sometimes horses need to rest, just like people do.

One stallion bites another.

The stallion takes care of the other horses in his band. He protects them. He often stands apart from the others, watching for predators.

Horses have many ways of grooming each other.

Horses in a band groom one another. Grooming helps to get rid of biting insects. Two horses stand side by side. Each one puts its head

Sometimes one horse cleans another's face by nibbling at it.

next to the other's tail. They use their tails to swish flies from each other's faces. When horses groom, they also nibble at one another's necks.

A mare (front) *is watching for danger. She protects her foal.*

Horses make sounds to each other.
The most common sound is the neigh (NAY).
A horse can hear a neigh from more than half
a mile away. Each horse sounds different.

Horses in a band know each other's sounds. A horse neighs if it gets lost from its band. Horses in the band neigh back. Then the lost horse knows where the band is.

Horses use sounds to send messages to each other.

A nicker is a soft, gentle sound. Horses greet each other with a nicker. Mares nicker to keep in touch with their foals.

The mare is looking back to check on her foal.

The stallion (front) *leads his band to safety.*

When a horse senses danger, it snorts to
warn the other horses in the band. The other
horses stop grazing. They get ready to run.
If the danger comes near, the band runs away.

These two stallions are fighting.

Sometimes stallions fight each other.
A young stallion may come to the band of an
older one. The young stallion might test the
strength of the older horse. At first, the two
stallions sniff one another. They neigh loudly.
They prance back and forth. Then they paw at
the ground with their front hooves.

Usually, the young stallion gives up. But if the band's stallion is weaker than the young stallion, the two horses may fight. The two stallions rear up on their hind legs. They strike at each other with their front hooves. They may try to bite each other's legs. Finally, one of the stallions gives up. It runs away.

When two horses fight, one is usually chased off.

Chapter 4

The mare is licking her new baby. At what time of year are foals usually born?

Raising Babies

 Mares give birth about once a year. Most foals are born in the spring. In the spring, it is warm. There is plenty of food for the horses to eat.

Foals nurse, or drink their mother's milk. When they are two or three weeks old, they try nibbling grass. After about six months, they no longer need their mother's milk.

This foal is nursing.

A mare watches as her foal tries to stand up.

A foal can stand up about 20 minutes after it is born. Soon it can run. Foals romp and play together. They grow quickly.

Foals begin to eat grass a few weeks after they are born.

A foal builds strong legs by running with its mother.

Young stallions live in the band until they are two or three years old. Then they go off to live together. This group of young stallions is called a bachelor (BATCH-luhr) band. A stallion stays in a bachelor band until he is about five years old. Then he is old enough to start his own band.

This foal is nuzzling its mother.

A foal stays near its mother when it runs with the band.

Young mares leave their band when they are about three or four years old. They join another band. Sometimes a bachelor stallion finds a young mare who has wandered away from her band. Then he and the mare start a new band.

Chapter 5

Most horses belong to people. How many kinds of wild horses are left?

People and Horses

Wild horses once lived across Europe, Asia, and North America. Just one kind of wild horse is left. It is called the Asian wild horse. It is an endangered species. Only a few of that kind of horse are still living.

Sometimes people use horses for rides through the countryside.

Only about 20 or 30 Asian wild horses remain wild. About 180 live in zoos. The other wild horses are extinct. When a kind of animal becomes extinct, there are none left.

Wild horses became extinct in North America a long time ago. Then people from Spain moved to Mexico and the American Southwest. They brought horses with them. Later, some horses escaped from people. The horses that escaped became feral horses.

Most horses live on farms or ranches. People take care of them.

Some farmers use horses for plowing fields.

For thousands of years, horses have worked hard for people. People used horses for getting from one place to another. And people used horses for farming, hunting, and sports. Trucks, cars, tractors, and machines take care of most of our needs now. But horses are still important to many people.

In the American West, cowboys still use horses to round up cattle. Some farmers use big, strong horses instead of tractors.

People also use horses in sports and games. Many people enjoy horseback riding, horse races, polo matches, jumping contests, and horse shows. And horses are friends to many people. Along with other animals like dogs and cats, horses can be people's best friends.

Jumping takes lots of practice for both the horse and the rider.

On Sharing a Book

As you know, adults greatly influence a child's attitude toward reading. When a child sees you read, or when you share a book with a child, you're sending a message that reading is important. Show the child that reading a book together is important to you. Find a comfortable, quiet place. Turn off the television and limit other distractions like telephone calls.

Be prepared to start slowly. Take turns reading parts of this book. Stop and talk about what you're reading. Talk about the photographs. You may find that much of the shared time is spent discussing just a few pages. This discussion time is valuable for both of you, so don't move through the book too quickly. If the child begins to lose interest, stop reading. Continue sharing the book at another time. When you do pick up the book again, be sure to revisit the parts you have already read. Most importantly, enjoy the book!

Be a Vocabulary Detective

You will find a word list on page 5. Words selected for this list are important to understanding the topic of this book. Encourage the child to be a word detective and search for the words as you read the book together. Talk about what the words mean and how they are used in the sentence. Do any of these words have more than one meaning? You will find these words defined in a glossary on page 46.

What about Questions?

Use questions to make sure the child understands the information in this book. Here are some suggestions:

> What did this paragraph tell us? What does this picture show? What do you think we will learn about next? What do you think it's like being a horse? How are horses like zebras? How are they different from zebras? Can horses see well? Can they hear well? What do horses eat? What do you like most about horses? What is your favorite part of the book? Why?

If the child has questions, don't hesitate to respond with questions of your own, such as: What do *you* think? Why? What is it that you don't know? If the child can't remember certain facts, turn to the index.

Introducing the Index

The index is an important learning tool. It helps readers get information quickly without searching throughout the whole book. Turn to the index on page 47. Choose an entry, such as *eating,* and ask the child to use the index to find out what horses eat. Repeat this exercise with as many entries as you like. Ask the child to point out the differences between an index and a glossary. (The index helps readers find information quickly, while the glossary tells readers what words mean.)

All the World in Metric!

Although our monetary system is in metric units (based on multiples of 10), the United States is one of the few countries in the world that does not use the metric system of measurement. Here are some conversion activities you and the child can do using a calculator:

WHEN YOU KNOW:	MULTIPLY BY:	TO FIND:
miles	1.609	kilometers
feet	0.3048	meters
inches	2.54	centimeters
gallons	3.787	liters
tons	0.907	metric tons
pounds	0.454	kilograms

Activities

Imagine being a horse. What would a day in a horse family be like? Make up a story about it. Draw pictures to go with your story.

Visit a zoo or a ranch where horses can be found. Spend some time watching them. During a five-minute time period, what do they do? How do they behave when they are by themselves? How do they behave in a group?

Make a horse book. Write down some interesting facts you learned from this book. Write down some facts about the horses you saw at the zoo. Add some information from other books to your horse book.

Glossary

band—a family of horses

breeds—kinds of horses

domesticated—tamed to live with people

endangered—having only a few of a kind of animal still living

extinct—having no members of a kind of animal still living

foal—a horse who is less than one year old

graze—to eat grass and other plants

herbivores (HUR-buh-vorz)—animals who eat only plants

hoof—a horse's foot

mane—a strip of coarse hair on top of a horse's neck

mare—an adult female horse

nurse—drink mother's milk

predators (PREH-duh-turz)—animals who hunt other animals for food

stallion (STAL-yun)—an adult male horse

Index

Pages listed in **bold** type refer to photographs.

The Early Bird Nature Books Series